ADVENTURES IN COLONIAL AMERICA

# THE FARM

## Life in Colonial Pennsylvania

by James E. Knight

illustrated by Karen Milone

Troll

*Cover art by Shi Chen.*

*Library of Congress Cataloging-in-Publication Data*

Knight, James E.
   The farm.

   Summary: An indentured servant looks back
on his five years of service on the farm of a
Pennsylvania German family in the 1760's.
   1. Pennsylvania—Social life and customs—
Colonial period, ca. 1600–1775—Juvenile
literature.   2. Farm life—Pennsylvania—
Juvenile literature. [1. Pennsylvania—Social
life and customs—Colonial period, ca. 1600–
1775.   2. Farm life—Pennsylvania.   3. Indentured servants.   4. United States—Social life
and customs—Colonial period, ca. 1600–1775]
I. Milone, Karen, ill.   II. Title.
F152.K65   974.7'02      81-23083
ISBN 0-89375-730-6 (lib. bdg.)    AACR2
ISBN 0-8167-4801-2 (pbk.)

This edition published 1998 by Troll Communications L.L.C.

Printed in the United States of America.

10  9  8  7  6  5  4  3  2

# THE FARM

*Life in Colonial Pennsylvania*

*October, 1766:* I, Thomas Ellison, celebrated my twenty-first birthday last month. It is hard to believe that I have been in America for five long years.

Yet here it is again—harvest time in Pennsylvania. I still marvel at how golden the rippling wheat fields look in this rich land of Lancaster County. It is so different from my father's farm in England. Soon we will be reaping these fields with our scythes. Then Master Mitteldorf, his sons, and I will thresh the wheat and store it in the Master's barn.

It will be my last harvest with these kind German folk. Next month I will be released from my indentured service. I will be a freed bondsman at last—free to farm my own land! But I know it will be hard to leave these people. They have been a family to me. Their sons, Karl and Klaus, are like brothers. And Anna, with her golden hair flying as she brings the eggs from the barn each morning...yes, a sister, of course. But more, too. Yet I dare not think of that now.

I remember the day five years ago, when Master Mitteldorf came to fetch me from the ship at Philadelphia.

I had nearly given up hope that anyone would buy my indenture. Because I had no money to pay for my passage to America, I had signed indenture papers in the captain's cabin before we sailed from Liverpool. This was my bond—my promise—to work as a servant in America. But first an employer would have to pay the captain $178 for my passage across the ocean.

After our ship reached Philadelphia, my despair grew daily. Every morning, employers would come aboard and look over the indentured people. Those with skills—blacksmiths, tailors, carpenters—were chosen quickly. Skilled workers are much needed in the American Colonies. They often serve shorter terms than mere laborers—two or three years, and then they are free. But what of me—Tom Ellison? No one seemed to wish to purchase the labor of a poor farm boy—even though I was willing to serve any master in America for a full seven years!

Finally, after two weeks, there were only eight of us left on board. Some of us were sick, and we feared that we would be sold to a "soul driver." For very little money, soul drivers would buy the labor of people no one else

wanted—the sick and the old. Then they auctioned them off like cattle in towns and villages. They were sellers of human souls.

But one morning, a man with a thick German accent came aboard the ship and inspected us. At last, he motioned to me, and we went to the captain's cabin. I learned that the man's name was Hans Mitteldorf and that he was a farmer. There was a twinkle in his blue eyes, and I found myself liking him immediately. The captain produced my indenture papers and began to talk.

"Ellison here is young and strong," said the captain, pointing to my bare arms. "He comes of good English farming stock. He knows the plow and the pitchfork."

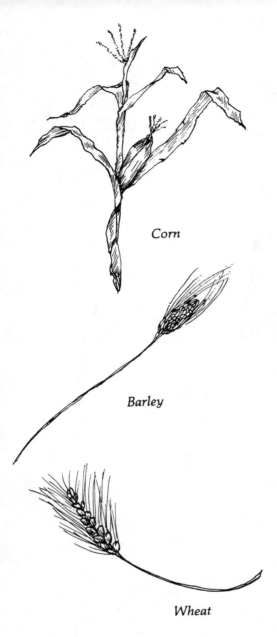

Corn

Barley

Wheat

"How many acres did you farm in England, young man?" Herr Mitteldorf asked.

"Fifty," I replied.

"I have three hundred," he said. "Even with two big sons I cannot begin to farm them all. I badly need another hand. Would you like to work on my farm in Lancaster County?"

I had no idea where Lancaster County was—but I said I would be most eager to go.

"Good," he said. "Captain, you may draw up the terms, and I shall purchase the boy's indenture. He shall serve for six years. At the end of that time, he shall be given an axe, a suit of clothes, fifty acres of my land at the north fence, and—well, whatever else a bondsman receives with his freedom. Are you agreeable to this, young man?"

I was. It was a most generous offer. I had dreamed of owning my own land someday and farming it myself. But I had expected to serve the usual full seven years!

8

One-handled Plow

Suddenly, just as he was about to sign my indenture papers, Herr Mitteldorf paused. My heart sank. Was he going to change his mind?

"Tell me, young man," he said slowly, "do you read and write English?"

I replied that I did.

"Good!" he said. "If you will instruct my children in English, I shall reduce the indenture to five years. Do you agree to these terms?"

I nodded. I could hardly believe my good fortune. Then my new employer signed my papers, put them in his pocket, and we left the ship.

So it was that I came to live and work on this farm in Pennsylvania. I have not regretted one minute of these five years. In England, on my father's farm, I thought I had learned well how to cultivate the land and live upon it. But these settlers have opened my eyes to new ways of farming.

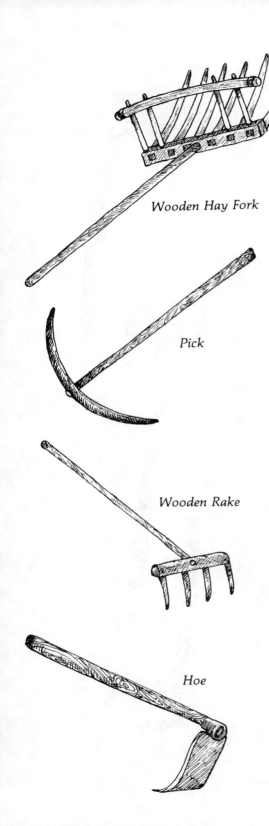

Wooden Hay Fork

Pick

Wooden Rake

Hoe

Instead of using the same field over and over until the soil is no longer good, the farmers here let each field lie fallow every few years. This means they do not plant anything on it. When they are ready to plant the field again, they fertilize it to replace some of the rich minerals it has lost. And they rotate the crops, too. They do not use the same field for the same crop year after year, as many other farmers do. By these methods, they produce more food per acre.

"Thomas," Herr Mitteldorf said to me during my first planting season, "this land is a gift, and we must take care of it. Some farmers use the soil until it is so poor and dry it has no more to give. Foolishly, they leave it, clear new fields, and then make the same mistake all over again. In the Colonies there is much wild and beautiful territory. But the day will come when there will be no new lands to move to—nothing but the old fields. Yes, Thomas, we must respect and care for the precious land."

I remember the first land I helped the Mitteldorfs clear. I had only been here a month or two. Although the Master owned three hundred acres, he had been able to farm only about a third of that rich land. With me here to help, he

decided to clear a few more acres of trees for planting.

So one morning we carried our axes to the woodlands beyond the far pasture. From what I had heard about colonial farming methods, I assumed we would bind the trees—make deep cuts around their trunks. This would kill the trees. Then, without the labor of cutting them down, we could plant crops between them.

But when the Mitteldorfs cleared the land, they chopped down the trees and dug up the roots. We worked very hard for several weeks, and when we were through, there was nothing left in the ground to damage the Master's sturdy wooden plow.

The new field would be for corn. The present corn field was not yielding a good crop, so for a season, the soil was to lie fallow. Then wheat, rye, or some other crop would be planted there.

I wondered what would be done with all the trees we had cut down. I soon found out. The Master, Karl, Klaus, and I set to work splitting fence rails and fashioning fence posts. The land we cleared had to be fenced off from the pastures nearby, where the horses, sheep, and cows grazed. Otherwise, the animals would get into the crops.

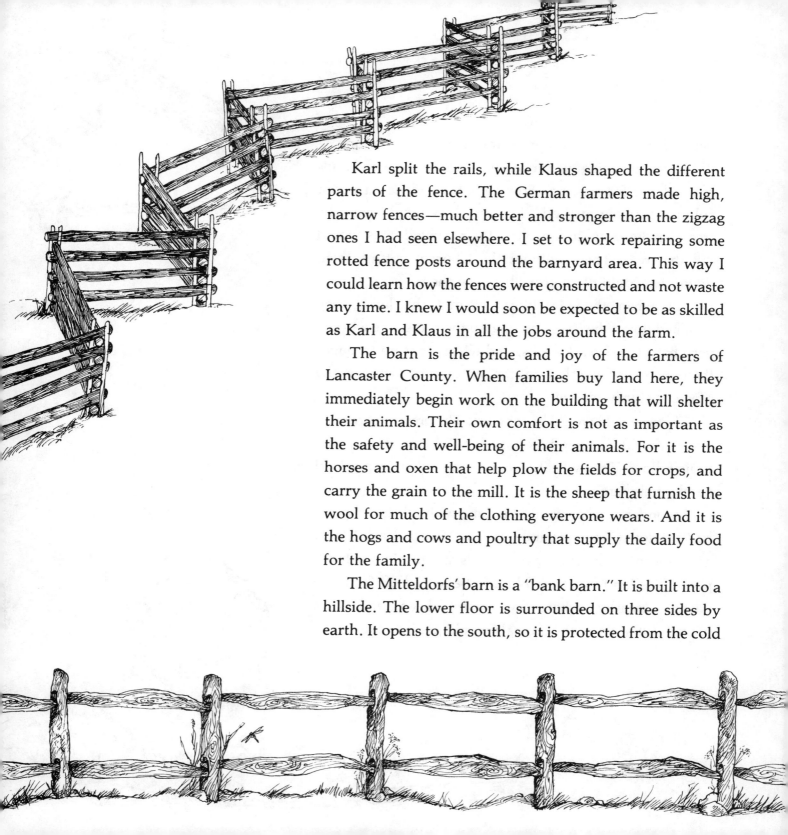

Karl split the rails, while Klaus shaped the different parts of the fence. The German farmers made high, narrow fences—much better and stronger than the zigzag ones I had seen elsewhere. I set to work repairing some rotted fence posts around the barnyard area. This way I could learn how the fences were constructed and not waste any time. I knew I would soon be expected to be as skilled as Karl and Klaus in all the jobs around the farm.

The barn is the pride and joy of the farmers of Lancaster County. When families buy land here, they immediately begin work on the building that will shelter their animals. Their own comfort is not as important as the safety and well-being of their animals. For it is the horses and oxen that help plow the fields for crops, and carry the grain to the mill. It is the sheep that furnish the wool for much of the clothing everyone wears. And it is the hogs and cows and poultry that supply the daily food for the family.

The Mitteldorfs' barn is a "bank barn." It is built into a hillside. The lower floor is surrounded on three sides by earth. It opens to the south, so it is protected from the cold

winter winds. All the animals are kept on this lower level. During freezing weather, snug in their stalls, the animals stay warm and healthy. Good farmers know that if an animal is kept warm, it will need less food.

13

The upper floor of the barn is the loft. On its northern, uphill side, the doors are wide enough for a hay wagon to be driven through. It is in the loft that we do the threshing of the grain crops—wheat, rye, oats, and barley—when the cold weather sets in.

Near the barnyard grows Mistress Mitteldorf's vegetable garden. The garden is an important part of the farm. The potatoes, carrots, and green vegetables grown here make up much of the family's food supply. If the geese ever get into the garden, they will do much damage. For this reason, they wear wooden yokes about their long necks, to prevent them from getting out of the barnyard.

Mistress Mitteldorf also grows a number of herbs in her garden. These are sometimes made into broths and herb teas, which are used for medicine. Once, when I had a toothache, Anna fixed me a mixture of herbs and butter.

14

Then she added a small amount of gunpowder! She told me to rub it on my gums, and the pain quickly went away.

Anna and the two boys are rarely sick. Indeed, Anna, with her rosy cheeks, is as fit and energetic as her cheerful mother. And this in spite of the fact that she works from early morning to evening. But everyone here works without grumbling, for there is much satisfaction in seeing the farm thrive and grow.

There are many pleasant times, too, with much laughter and good fun. All the neighbors help one another at harvest time, traveling from one farm to another in large groups. When the work is done, there is always a big meal. Then the neighbors gather to visit and sing. Cornhusking time, in particular, is a happy time.

I will never forget one cornhusking bee. It was during my third year in America. I was sitting between Karl and Anna. We were all singing, as we steadily pulled the husks off the corn. Suddenly, Karl poked me in the ribs and pointed to the ear of corn I was holding.

"Look, Tom!" he cried. "You have found an ear of corn with red kernels. Now you must kiss the girl next to you. It is the custom."

I leaned over and quickly kissed Anna on the cheek. Everyone roared with laughter and clapped their hands.

Indeed, the cornhusking bees of harvest time are festive days. But they are also very important days, for the farm's corn crop is highly valued. The Master's most important crops are wheat and rye. He grows barley and oats, too—as well as corn. Much of the corn is used to feed the animals. The grain that is to be ground into meal and flour for the family's use is taken in a horse-drawn wagon to Hofstader's Mill, nearby.

16

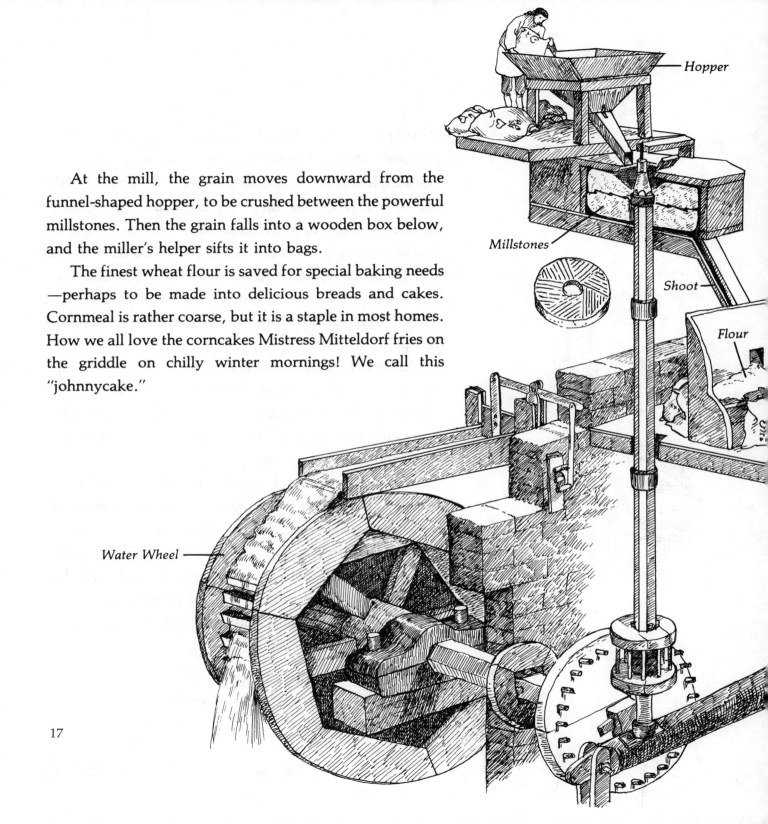

At the mill, the grain moves downward from the funnel-shaped hopper, to be crushed between the powerful millstones. Then the grain falls into a wooden box below, and the miller's helper sifts it into bags.

The finest wheat flour is saved for special baking needs —perhaps to be made into delicious breads and cakes. Cornmeal is rather coarse, but it is a staple in most homes. How we all love the corncakes Mistress Mitteldorf fries on the griddle on chilly winter mornings! We call this "johnnycake."

Hopper

Millstones

Shoot

Flour

Water Wheel

When the crops have been good, extra grain is taken by Herr Mitteldorf to a merchant miller near the city of Philadelphia. This is a much larger mill, and here the Master receives cash for his grain. Lancaster County deserves its name as a "bread colony," for it sends a great deal of flour to Philadelphia. Along with salted pork and beef from Pennsylvania farms, some of the flour is then shipped to the southern colonies—where it is exchanged for rice. The rest of the flour is sent to the West Indies and Europe.

At harvest time, the men swing heavy scythes through the stalks of waving wheat. This is one of the hardest farm jobs of all. The women and children also leave their daily chores to come into the fields. They bind the cut stalks into bundles called sheaves.

The next step of the harvest is threshing the grain. It is an itchy, messy job. When the cold weather comes, we spread the sheaves on the barn floor and beat them to knock the grains off the stalks. Next we gather up the straw, which will be used for the animals' stalls. Finally, we must take the remaining mixture of grain and bits of straw up to the loft and winnow it—so that the grains will be separated from the chaff.

After my first two harvests with the Mitteldorfs, I was allowed to go with Karl to Hofstader's Mill. Then, after the third harvest, the Master called me to him and said, "Tom, this year you will take the grain to Hofstader's to be milled." I was greatly touched by this—and proud. It showed that he trusted me—an indentured servant—with the fruits of his hard labor.

Some masters take cruel advantage of their servants, and treat them as slaves. Indentured workers can be forced to labor at any task—for any number of hours a day. I had heard of one boy who was beaten regularly by his master. Once he had tried to run away, but was soon found. After that, his master had an iron collar welded around the boy's neck. This meant that he was a runaway servant and was to be treated with suspicion wherever he went.

On my way home from the mill, I passed what the Mitteldorfs called the "old house." It was the first house built by my master's father, Jakob Mitteldorf, when he came here from Germany to settle in 1711. It was his home

for many years—until he and his only son built the present farmhouse with its thick fieldstone walls. The "old house" is really a large log cabin. Today it is used as a storeroom for tools and grain.

One thing about the "old house" has always fascinated me. On the roof is an iron figure of an Indian. It is a sign that Jakob Mitteldorf paid the Indians for his land, and therefore, they should not attack his family. I have seen Indians pass occasionally, point at the iron figure—and nod with satisfaction.

In my years with the Mitteldorfs, I believe I have enjoyed the winters the most. These are quiet, happy times. In the main room of the farmhouse, we sit around a roaring fire. Sometimes we sing, for music is much appreciated. But I also use the winter months to teach English grammar and spelling to Anna, Karl, and Klaus. The Master and Mistress listen carefully and learn, too. German is still spoken in most homes here in Lancaster County—however, the people are eager to read and write in English. There are some small community schools. But most families believe that the children's most important task is to learn how to farm—so often they do not spend much time at their lessons.

During the winter, when I am not teaching, I am likely to be repairing broken tools with Karl and Klaus. The Master works on his fine gunstocks, and Mistress Mitteldorf and her daughter are always busy making new clothes or patching and mending old clothes. On a Pennsylvania farm, almost everything is made from scratch, and nothing is thrown away until it can no longer be used.

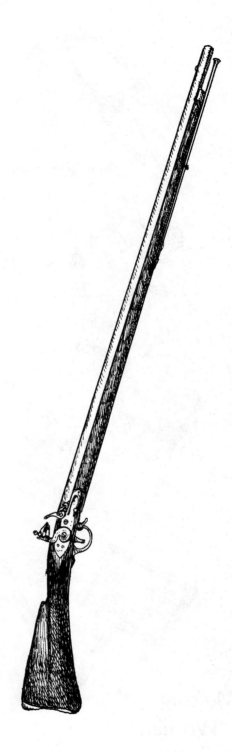

*Shearing the Sheep*

Every girl learns how to spin fibers into thread. The yarn comes from sheep's wool and from the flax that is grown on the farm. After it is spun, it must be woven into cloth on a large loom. Linen cloth is made from the flax, woolen cloth from the sheep's wool. And from the cloth, the women and girls make shirts, pants, dresses, and petticoats, as well as sheets and blankets. For cold weather, they weave linsey-woolsey cloth, which is a mixture of linen and wool yarn.

*Carding
the Wool*

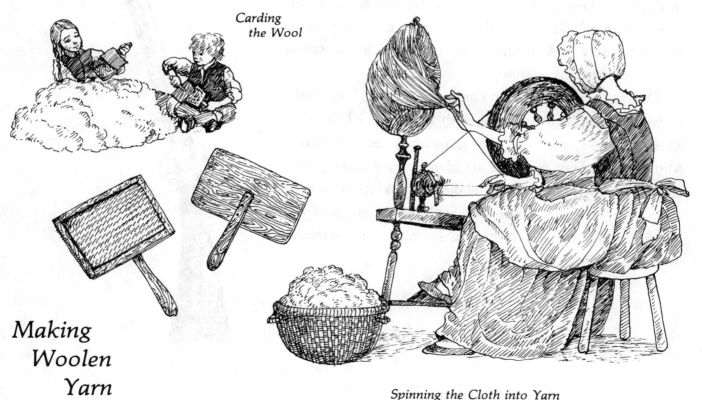

# Making Woolen Yarn

*Spinning the Cloth into Yarn*

Cutting the Flax

# Making Linen

Breaking the
Sheaths of Flax

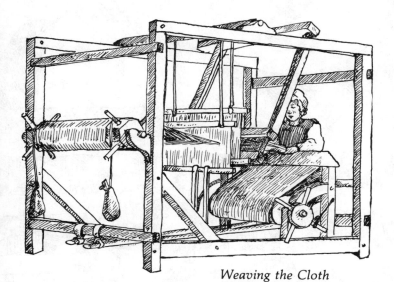

Weaving the Cloth

Cleaning the Flax

Combing the Flax with a Hatchel

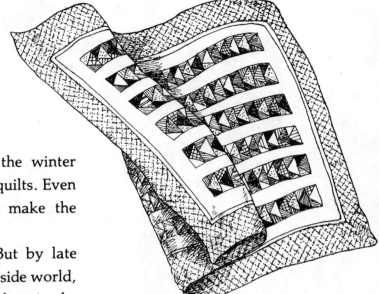

The Mistress and Anna especially love the winter evenings when neighbors join them in making quilts. Even little girls sew, their fingers flying as they make the colorful patchwork patterns.

Yes, the winter is a busy time for all. But by late March, we begin to long for news from the outside world, for fresh fruits and vegetables, and for long days in the sunshine. Mistress Mitteldorf's preserves and jellies are gone. The root cellar is empty, for we have eaten the last of the potatoes and carrots and dried apples that were stored there.

When spring finally comes, we are ready. The tools have been repaired. The new lambs and calves and piglets are eager to nibble the first green shoots coming up out of the ground.

Now the fields must be plowed, and then harrowed, or leveled, to receive the seed. When the new seeds are finally planted, everyone rejoices—for once again, the crops are safely in the rich black earth.

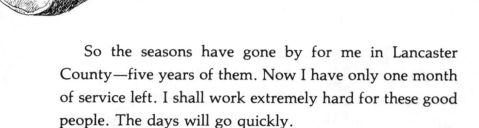

So the seasons have gone by for me in Lancaster County—five years of them. Now I have only one month of service left. I shall work extremely hard for these good people. The days will go quickly.

*November, 1766:* I cannot quite believe it! I have become a freed bondsman at last!

On that important morning one week ago, I felt as if I were in some strange dream. I was seated on one of the Master's horses. The Mitteldorfs were all around me, wishing me well. They had given me a horse to help me clear my new land. In my knapsack were two smoked hams, which Karl and Klaus had given me. Anna had knitted me a new muffler for the winter. And I was dressed in a new suit of linsey-woolsey. Mistress Mitteldorf had worked on it for weeks in secret. Also in my knapsack were a fine, sharp axe and a pitchfork. I would be needing them both on my new land. Truly, was I not the luckiest of men?

The Master reached up and shook my hand.

28

"So, Tom," he said. "You have worked hard—like my own sons. Go now and work your own land—you have earned it. Cut down trees and build a strong cabin. When you are ready, we shall come by and help you raise the roof."

Then, with a twinkle in his eye, he said, "And maybe you'll be needing a wife soon."

Karl and Klaus doubled up with laughter. Anna was blushing. Quickly, I turned the mare's head north and started off. When I stopped and looked back, Anna was still waving.

I am indeed a happy man. I am ready to make *my* start in America.

# Index

*(Page numbers that appear in **boldface** type refer to illustrations.)*